snapshot·picture·library

BIRDS

snapshot·picture·library

BIRDS

FOG CITY PRESS

Published by Fog City Press,
a division of Weldon Owen Inc.
814 Montgomery Street
San Francisco, CA 94133
www.weldonowen.com

WELDON OWEN GROUP
Chief Executive Officer John Owen
Chief Financial Officer Simon Fraser

WELDON OWEN INC.
President, Chief Executive Officer Terry Newell
Vice President, International Sales Stuart Laurence
Vice President, Sales & Marketing Amy Kaneko
Vice President, Publisher Roger Shaw
Vice President, Creative Director Gaye Allen
Managing Editor Karen Penzes
Assistant Editor Sonia Vallabh
Art Director Kelly Booth
Designer Andreas Schueller
Design Assistant Justin Hallman
Production Director Chris Hemesath
Production Manager Michelle Duggan
Sales Manager Emily Bartle
Color Manager Teri Bell

Text Maria Behan
Picture Research Andy Sir

A WELDON OWEN PRODUCTION
© 2007 Weldon Owen Inc.

Library of Congress Control Number: 2007936041

ISBN-13: 978-1-74089-642-9
ISBN-10: 1-74089-642-4

10 9 8 7 6 5 4 3 2 1

Color separations by Sang Choy International, Singapore.
Printed by Tien Wah Press in Singapore.

If you go outside or even look out the window, you'll probably see a bird. And if you go some place far away, like the rain forests or the South Pole, you'll find them there, too.

The places where they live and the things that they eat make every kind of bird different. Most fly, but a few, like penguins, don't. Some are almost as small as bugs, but a few are even taller than you. Birds can be as different as people are.

Birds can make things look bright, even when the world seems gray.

Baby birds are fed by their parents, who bring them berries, nectar— and sometimes wiggly worms!

Birds have families, just like us. Males and females sometimes stay together for life—and parents take good care of their babies.

One of the best places to look for birds is way up in the trees.

But you'll find hummingbirds hanging around flowers, since that's where they find their favorite food.

When they fly, hummingbirds' tiny wings beat really fast—up to 80 times a second—and they can fly backward, too!

You'll find other birds hanging
out where we do—in parks,
yards, and even on city streets.

But some of
the fanciest
birds live in
rain forests.

Birds spend most of their time looking for food. Most of them see much better than us!

Great eyesight, speed, and strength make birds like eagles and hawks very good hunters.

Bald eagles have white heads—not bald ones! They live near lakes, rivers, or the sea because fish are their favorite food.

Eagles, like most birds, have eyes on the sides of their heads. But these owls are like us: their eyes are in the front.

Many sea birds have long beaks. Pelicans have the longest of all—so long they have to rest them on their backs when they sleep.

Long beaks help
shorebirds catch
their dinner—fish!

Baby ducks follow the first moving thing they see once they come out of their egg. Usually, that's their mom—but if it's you, they'll follow you!

Penguins have flippers instead of wings—way better for swimming!

Other birds that live near the water do have wings, but they're still great at swimming or diving for food!

Like lots of other seabirds, gulls often fly in a group, because traveling like that saves energy.

Storks and
herons have
long skinny
legs too—less
to carry around
when they fly!

Ostriches and emus also have long legs—and long necks to match! They are too big and heavy to fly.

Birds like vultures mostly eat animals that have been dead for awhile. It sounds icky, but not if you think of them as nature's clean-up crew!

The parrot's sharp beak helps it
crack seeds, while the hornbill's
long one helps it catch bugs.

Toucans use their beaks to pick berries and to get other toucans to notice them. With beaks like that, they're sure hard to miss!

Birds' feathers come in lots of beautiful colors. With their brightly colored feathers, parrots are like jewels in the forest.

Just like people, birds can be as different as the places they live.

Which birds
have you
spotted where
you live?

Peacock
Southeast Asia

Sparrow
Europe, Africa, Asia

Yellow Rumped Warbler
Eastern North America

Great Spotted Woodpecker
Europe and Northern Asia

Mountain Bluebird
Western North America

Broad-Tailed Hummingbird
Western North America

Emperor Penguins
Antarctica

Ruby-Throated Hummingbird
Eastern North America

Bateleur Eagle
Sub-Saharan Africa

Cardinal
The Americas

Hummingbird
The Americas

Golden Eagle
North America, Europe, Asia

Tufted Titmouse
Eastern Canada and eastern United States

Blue-Chested Hummingbird
South America

Harris's Hawk
Southern North America and parts of South America

Rufous Hummingbird
Western North America

Hummingbird
The Americas

Bald Eagle
North America

European Magpies
Europe, Asia, northern Africa

Starlings
Europe, Asia, Africa and Australia

Barn Owl
Worldwide except Antarctica

European Bee-Eater
Europe, parts of Africa and Asia

European Robin
Europe and parts of Asia and Africa

Snowy Owl
Northern Canada, Europe, and Asia

Great Tit
Europe and Asia

Rufous Hummingbird
Western North America

Great Horned Owl
The Americas

Eastern Bluebird
Eastern North America and parts of Central America

Common Kingfisher
Europe, Asia, Africa

Brown Pelican
Coasts of North and South America

Blue Jay
United States and southern Canada

Woodland Kingfisher
Tropical Africa

Little Black Cormorant
Australia

Black-Tailed Godwit
Europe and Asia

 White Stork
Europe, Asia, and Africa

 Mallard Duckling
Worldwide

 Green-Winged Teal Ducklings
North America

 Mute Swan Cygnet
Europe and Asia

 Emperor Penguins
Antarctica

 Adelie Penguin
Antarctica and nearby islands

 Adelie Penguin
Antarctica and nearby islands

 Canada Goose
North America

 Albatross and Petrel
Southern hemisphere

 Jackdaw
Europe, Asia, and northwest Africa

 Seagulls
Coastal regions

 Laughing Gull and Sanderlings
Western North America

 Sandhill Crane
North America, northeastern Siberia

 White Stork
Europe, Asia, and Africa

 Great White Pelican
Asia, Africa, and southeastern Europe

 Great Blue Heron
North and Central America, West Indies

 Ostrich
Africa

 Ostrich
Africa

 King Vulture
Southern Mexico to northern Argentina

 Macaw
Mexico, Central and South America

 Southern Ground Hornbill
Africa

 Toco Toucan
Central and eastern South America

 Green-Winged Macaws
The Americas

 Sun Conures
South America

 Eastern Rosella
Southeast Australia and Tasmania

 Saddle-Billed Stork
Sub-Saharan Africa

 Atlantic Puffin
Northern Europe, Iceland, eastern North America

 Caribbean Flamingo
Parts of South America, Mexico, and the Caribbean

 Green Violet-Eared Hummingbird
Central and South America

 Blue Tit
Europe and western Asia

 Peacock
Southeast Asia

European Bee-Eater
Europe, parts of Africa and Asia

ACKNOWLEDGMENTS

Weldon Owen would like to thank the following people for their assistance in the production of this book: Diana Heom, Ashley Martinez, Danielle Parker, Lucie Parker, Phil Paulick, and Erin Zaunbrecher.

CREDITS

Key t=top; b=bottom; DT=Dreamstime; iSP=iStockphoto; LO=Lucky Oliver; SST=Shutterstock

2 DT; **5** iSP; **6** iSP; **8** SST; **10**t, b iSP; **11** SST; **12** DT; **13**t, b iSP; **14** SST; **15**t, b iSP; **16**t, b iSP; **17** SST; **18** SST; **20** DT; **21** iSP; **22**t, b iSP; **23** SST; **24**t, b iSP; **25** iSP; **26** iSP; **27** SST; **28** SST; **30**t, b iSP; **31** iSP; **32** SST; **33**t SST, b DT; **35** SST; **36**t SST, b iSP; **37** iSP; **38** iSP; **39**t, b iSP; **40** iSP; **41**t, b iSP; **42** SST; **43** SST; **44** SST; **46** iSP; **47**t SST, b iSP; **48** iSP; **49** SST; **50** SST; **52** SST; **53** iSP; **55** iSP; **56** SST; **57**t SST, b LO; **58** iSP; **59** SST; **60** iSP; **61**t, b iSP; **64** DT.